THE SILENCE LIVING IN HOUSES

Esther Morgan was born in Kidderminster, Worcester-shire. She first started writing poetry while working as a volunteer at the Wordsworth Trust in Grasmere, Cumbria. After completing an MA in Creative Writing at the University of East Anglia in 1997, she taught on UEA's undergraduate creative writing course and for the Department of Continuing Education. During her time at UEA she edited four editions of the poetry anthology *Reactions*.

As well as freelance teaching and editing she helped set up The Poetry Archive, the world's largest online collection of poets reading their own work, working as the site's Historic Recordings Manager for several years: www.poetryarchive.org.

She received an Eric Gregory Award in 1998, and her first collection, *Beyond Calling Distance*, was published by Bloodaxe in 2001. It won the Aldeburgh First Collection Prize and was shortlisted for the John Llewellyn Rhys Prize. Her second collection, *The Silence Living in Houses* (Bloodaxe Books, 2005), was largely inspired by her time caretaking a run-down Edwardian house in Goring-on-Thames, Oxfordshire. In 2010 she won the Bridport Poetry Prize for her poem 'This Morning', included in her third collection *Grace* (Bloodaxe Books, 2011), a Poetry Book Society Recommendation, which was shortlisted for the T.S. Eliot Prize. Her fourth collection, *The Wound Register* (Bloodaxe Books, 2018), was runner-up for the 2019 New Angle Prize for Literature and shortlisted for the poetry category of the East Anglian Book Awards 2018.

After four years in Oxfordshire she moved back to Norfolk where she lives with her husband and daughter and currently works for Norfolk Museums Service.

ESTHER MORGAN

The Silence Living
in Houses

BLOODAXE BOOKS

ISBN: 978 1 85224 711 9

First published 2005 by
Bloodaxe Books Ltd,
Eastburn,
South Park,
Hexham,
Northumberland NE46 1BS.

www.bloodaxebooks.com
For further information about Bloodaxe titles
please visit our website and join our mailing list
or write to the above address for a catalogue.

Supported using public funding by
**ARTS COUNCIL
ENGLAND**

Digital reprint of the 2005 Bloodaxe Books edition.

For my grandmother then, and for Kelvyn now

'So a house is not the same for a woman. She is not someone who walks into the house, to make use of it and will walk out again. She is the house; there is no separation possible.'

ALICE MUNRO (from her short story 'The Office')

ACKNOWLEDGEMENTS

Acknowledgements are due to the editors of the following pub-
lications where some of these poems first appeared: *Envoi*,
Mslexia, *Poetry Life*, *Poetry London*, *The Rialto*, www.nth-
position.com. A sequence of ten poems received a Special
Commendation in the Writers Inc 2004 Writers of the Year
Competition.

This collection would not have been completed without
the advice and support of family and friends. In particular
I'd like to thank: Moniza Alvi and the Poetry School group,
John Burnside, Polly Clark, Helen Cross, Brian Foster, Bridget
Gardner, Anna Garry, Jane Griffiths, Helen Ivory, Kerry
Keys, Carmina McConnell, Victoria Millar, Patrick Neil,
Helen Oswald, Fiona Robyn, David Staig, George and
Clarissa Szirtes, Morgan Yasbincek and Miranda Yates, all
of whom have encouraged and helped in many different
ways. I'd like to express my thanks and love to my parents
whose house has always been safe, and to Kelvyn for the
last twelve years.

CONTENTS

1

The House Of

The House Of

They come into their own at night
when the house is plumbed with darkness,
tapping at these ribs of lath and plaster,
the birthmarks of roses
like doctors testing a heart.

They are listening for the nameless:
a chinese-whispering of dust,
skin over a hollowness
where dreams might be spirited away
like dolls nested stiffly in lace.

This is the hour for secret christenings,
for trying to save those who are lost:
Lily   Ivy   Violet
called after flowers that once lined these walls,
their shade-loving faces.

Endurance

It was the photographer who risked his life,
who dived the expedition wreck
to bring back faces to the light,
their glass transparencies.

On the other side of the world
the women turned in again for winter
storing their sweetness
like the bulbs they wrapped in newspaper
to save them from frost.

Keepers of locked rooms and skeleton keys
they knew how to put a house to sleep,
layering linen with lavender,
swaddling silver against tarnish,
stowing away.

On nights when breath is visible
I listen to timbers creaking
like a seized ship:
the house rigged in ice and going down.

Domestic

Under the chestnut trees it's already night
as I turn back towards the house
where lights are coming on
though some of the windows
are still dark as mouths.

I'm carrying a bowl of blackberries
shiny and inscrutable as eyes.
I must have been picking them blind –
my arms are cross-hatched by scratches,
fingers stained to the knuckle-bones.

Her arms ache with the weight of the day's ashes,
though she's stealing this moment in the service
of herself; to stand at the sash
watching dusk harvesting the garden,
the moon rising like a flood inside her skin.

I am beginning to unsettle myself,
each step I take through long grass
a ghost's trespass on the living,
her face behind the glass encased
like a polished silver dish.

Before I sleep I will preserve this sweetness,
leave it cooling under muslin in the scullery,
refining and thickening like blood
as the oven ticks and contracts;
a secret recipe got by heart.

In the small hours a woman will wake
sat at a table so highly waxed
she will see her face in it –
the shock of wildness in her eyes,
the seeds caught between her teeth.

Self-possession

I am making a ghost for this house
so I can sleep safe at night,
her footsteps light on the stairs
answering the disconnected bells.

She will be pale of course, and thin
like a peeled switch of hazel,
quick and almost invisible
to the uninitiated

who will dismiss her
as a mouse
scuttling behind the skirting,
as a trick of nightshade and fever.

But I will believe in her
leaving the room just as I enter,
her presence implicit in drawn velvet curtains,
a different arrangement of dust.

Tonight, I can feel her
in this incipient headache:
she is coming, my less than familiar,
hot with impatience to exist.

Bone China

I want to leave something behind
like the maid who cracked one night
the length of her heart,
who crept shaking down the staircase
to where the service shone on the dresser,
plates pale as a row of moons.

She stacked them in her arms –
a weight greater than all she owned –
bore their white tower to the kitchen garden
where she stood between the soft fruit beds
and smashed each one against the wall
with a planetary anger.

That dawn she walked out of her story forever,
though her flavour salted the servants' tongues for months,
and clearing the ground a hundred years later
of this self-seeded scrub of ash
I can still piece bits of her together – white and sharp –
as if the earth were teething.

Codicil

To be left to myself:
like these antique roses and hidden beds,
the broken apple tree's distracted snow,
cow parsley smocking the dusk
intimate as petticoats.

To be beyond rescue:
like the woman with the pressed-flower face
who pushes through this wilderness
past the conservatory's sinking ship
into the rising tide of grasses.

Ghost-writing

I have never seen a ghost,
though it's whispered that the spirits
do have secrets to impart. I too
have wondered at the crying in the dark.

That's why I've invented her,
dressed her in the customary white –
my grandmother's shift of broderie anglais –
set her wandering the house at night.

How else am I to lay myself to rest?
Though I still wake bent over the page
deciphering a message in a shaky hand –
Don't breathe a word of this.

The Ghost of This House

The ghost of this house
is forgetting to believe in me
despite the feathers I hold to my lips,
the hearts drawn in the mist
of breathed-on windows.

She misses the evidence laid out
for her to find – a strand of hair on a pillowcase,
tell-tale tissue kisses in the bin,
my fingers printing the white walls
with forensic blossom.

Nothing impinges –
my existence hinges on a draught
angled through a half-open door,
her shoulder-blades' slight shiver
as she walks through me.

At night I make myself scarce,
haunting the edges of the darkness
she is mistress of, lost
in the muted television's
occasional light snow.

When she's asleep, I seat myself
at her dressing-table's triptych
tilting the mirrors this way and that,
trying to catch in the infinity of rooms
the flit of a face.

Perhaps I'm only the complex
origami of her dream – my flimsy skin
is becoming less convincing,
I worry at my argument of bone,
unnerved to detect

in this slow diminishment
a sense of coming home:
content to step aside in the empty kitchen,
to make room for the still life of knives,
the proved bread.

Half Sister

I watch you from my dark house,
how the sun tilts your face towards me,
your smile blossoming in the warmth.

I leave this house rarely
wrapped in white layers like a bee-keeper
to protect me from the swarms of light,

or like the veiled princess
whose throat was so translucent
the swallowed wine showed through.

Do you sense the thinness of my skin,
how, exposed, it would simmer like milk?
Do I arouse a cruelty in you or tenderness?

Last night I offered my sleeplessness to you,
my body glowing like a candle
under the magnolia's gloved hands.

Small-boned

Petite was the word to describe her –
a name like a pet on pearly feet,
a pat on the head,
treats held up just out of reach.

She pulled dry wishbones on Sundays
with her little finger – a shy snap,
the sound she imagined
her heart would make, breaking.

Fairy cakes – on tiptoe for the ingredients
in the high cupboards. Neighbours' compliments
Light as a feather! She beat air
into her sponge mix furiously,

thought of the honeycombed skeletons of birds,
the sweets she denied herself –
crumbling flakes, crunchies, the bubbles
that weighed so little.

She wore jackets with nipped-in waists,
stilettos that caught in gratings
(the feel of a heel once in her hand like a knife).
They tapped her secret fears along the pavement

like the girl in sugar-stiff petticoats
who knocks at her frosted window
small as a mouse after midnight,
not wanting to wake the dead.

Mouse-trap

She dusts the skirting of the larder
with flour before she goes to bed,
where she listens to her ivory bones knitting,
her blood unravelling in the dark.

In the morning, her dreams evaporate
like mist. Up first, she discovers
the network of patterns in the kitchen –
fretted paw-prints, white as a ghost's –

which she traces for a minute
then sweeps away, pretends they've never existed,
despite the nibbled biscuits,
the tiny teeth marks in the butter.

House-breaking

And when I put my mind to it
how easy it would be
to tear this house apart.

I'd buy the hardware:
axe and hammer – pick and sledge and claw –
the white plaster caving in like skulls.

No more sleepless nights – the intermittent
drip feed of its cry
driving me insane.

I'd rather have a roof of sky,
wind knifing through these rooms,
rain pouring in

so long as I might find its wasted skin,
the hair-lined bones,
something I could bury or name.

Fast

Since then everyone's been searching for answers,
and though nobody knew them, not really, the sisters,
we share what we've gleaned:

the taxi driver from their final trip into town
who watched the three of them sat like in church –
grave, stiff-backed, harking to something;

the woman who found them, her voice at the inquest a whisper
describing the icons and guttering candles, the one who died last
prostrate by the back door, key in her hand.

Sometimes, undressing for bed, I picture them –
giddy and blind and lighter than girls, locked up all summer
inside a house that mirrors my own.

Once I passed by their door in the evening,
heard some old jazz being played very quietly –
a curtain fluttered into the street like a veil.

Poppies

I disturbed the earth
and they put forth;
flagrant, pentecostal,
their gorgeous skirts flaring
too close to the walls.

At night I hasp my windows fast
against their silk incitement,
the ruffled flamenco
dancing in my staked
and tended bed.

They forget themselves,
how soon the wind will rattle
their balding heads,
how quickly they'll burn down
to a black and scatterable dust:

seeds so fine
I could hold in my fist
a field of blood.
Meantime, I'll starve it out
this scarlet fever,

though if you came home now
you would find me
parched as gorse:
a touch could be the torch
to set me blazing.

Mistress

There's always been someone to hide
inside hollow walls and sliding oak panels:
a divine of the heretic religion,
the family simpleton with their mooning face.

I used to frighten myself at midnight feasts
telling tales of nuns sealed up in cells
for devotion's sake, or some unspeakable sin.
When I slept, my eyes closed over their bones.

Every house contains a room that doesn't exist
where we find ourselves almost at home
behind this skim of horsehair plaster,
the roses breathing into your ear.

Care-taking

I keep everything in its place
from the lace wings and moths that flake the sills
to the husk of a mouse outside your door,
(though the cat that caught it is long since dust).

The curtains continue to fade, velvet tattering like antlers,
the walls slough off their paper like snakes.
The rooms look as they must in our absence;
leached of desire, empty as a guest room chair,
this glass vase rimed and flowerless.

As for myself I feel airy and winged like a seed;
it's as if I've already been shed
like my bedside rose in its circle of petals.
(You always said there was nothing of me.)

I make my last round at midnight
checking there's rust in the lock, the bolt's driven home.
I perform my duties as though you were watching,
touching each bar of the window
with hands as clean as the moon.

House-keeping

You do your work in the small hours
when I am most deeply asleep,
festooning the ceilings with cobwebs,
clouding my mirrors with dust.

You sprinkle mud over the rugs,
breathe tarnish into the silverware.
In the pure shimmer of damask
rings of red wine appear.

When mist rises like the ghost of milk
you melt up the backstairs
to gas-mantled attics
where you thin into air

though I know you've been keeping this house
by the cold that I wake to,
the ashes laid in my hearth,
this silence that shifts for itself.

2

The Silence Living in Houses

Boarding House

Though you've forgotten those rooms exist
your body remembers, your haunted blood:

At night your heart beats its fist against the wall,
your spine buzzes like a jar of wasps,

the sharp cry lodged inside your cortex
is working its way into your mouth.

House-bound

You wake bricked up inside his house
surrounded by a sea of wheat
with nothing to speak of between you
and the Urals, and no one around for miles
should you come to grief.

Instead you learn to read the sky
in his part of the world,
how a storm rises in the east,
comes plundering towards you through the fields
until it bursts right over your head
in a volley of thunder and hail.

You should leave in the night
as the monks once did,
carry your incorruptible body
until you reach the snows of the pass,
then bury it under a mountain.

House Rules

They are absolute.
They are mandarin.
Sometimes merely folding a sheet
or making a bed
is to break them.

For instance there's a right way
and a wrong way
to clear up this mess –
the spattered walls,
the tongues of broken china.

Which is which?
You spend the evening trying to guess
as you wait for his verdict,
hands resting on the table
like meat thawing for dinner.

Tonight he addresses your flesh –
Look what you made me do he says
as a flight of stairs
throws you full length,
a door walks into your face.

Her Given Names

At the word *cat*
she's down on all fours
performing her hunger,
warping and wefting through his legs,
arching her spine at his creamy voice.

Next he says *bitch* and in an instant
she's cringy and thin as a whippet,
ribs within range of his kick,
shivery with guilt, though she can't tell
what it is she's done.

Snake makes her hateful to herself,
cold and coiled in their bed,
eyes unblinking through the long night,
thoughts venomous –
by morning she'll have swallowed the dark.

She tries hard to change herself,
whispering *tiger, eagle, grizzly*
at the mirror, but each time she jumps
out of her skin, she hears him
calling her given name,

feels his gentle fingers
helping her climb back in,
zipping up her clingy flesh
(his favourite dress),
boned too tight to breathe.

Speciality

You know these cruel delicacies of old –
a mixture of the connoisseur's acquired taste
and the clever schoolboy's concocted torture:
the songbird drowned in cognac, trussed and roasted whole,
an oyster swallowed like a living tongue.

Once you watched him choose a lobster from the jostling tank,
its claws bound by elastic bands,
explaining as he did so that the famous scream
is only steam escaping from the shell,
that the creature itself feels nothing.

Feeling nothing has become your speciality,
though what he feels you can only guess:
Love is what the farmer always claims,
his rough hands stroking grain
down the long white throat.

Life on Earth

You know this is the species' binding ritual
by the glazed expression of the groomed,
the way they sit transfixed
like carvings on an ancient temple
while nails hard as horn
work their bodies inch by inch.

Close-up of a yawning Alpha male
lips peeled back from gums
of a shocking baby pink.
Your skin crawls back into the jungle
from where it came – huge nicotined teeth
unsheathe inside your head.

Specimen

(from a description in Mutants *by Armand Leroi)*

You might leave your body to medical science
like the man whose skeleton ran wild,
whose every bruise and injury
healed into bone
until the whole machinery of joint and tendon
seized inside a cage of pain –

his back fused to a sheet of bone,
his limbs, his neck, his hips distorted
by a slow accretion like a coral reef:
his jaw locked a year before he died.

You've seen his remains in a museum,
his original frame a ghost
encased in the lacy growths,
the bridges, struts and pinnacles of trauma.

When they open you up you wonder if they'll find,
beneath the later hardening,
the form that once existed
before you were twisted out of true:
the silvery femurs of a child,
the soft plates of a baby's moon-like skull.

Removals

Strange how after a year
there's always this box stamped FRAGILE
you haven't got round to unpacking,
furred with dust in the spare room.

When you lift it up it's light
as if all it could contain
are sheets of tissue paper, blisters of bubble-wrap –
the skins you use to protect what's breakable.

This time he stows it in the loft
where the insulation sleeps like snow.
And you know he's right when he tells you
if it were vital you'd have missed it by now,

you would be lying here in bed
with half a mind on mice – white teeth
shredding the darkness, weaving a nest
in the heart of it: pink, squirming, blind.

House of Mirrors

One morning you will wake
to find the mirrors of this house
empty and intact,
your bad thoughts decanted
quietly inside your skull.

You won't recall
the woman standing naked in the dark,
the broken skin, the bad luck,
lips it would be dangerous
to kiss a wrist with.

But for now it is still night
and no time for you to face
the oval of ice in the garden,
the girl who walks across its glitter
to stamp on the moon.

Imperative

This morning don't go down to the kitchen
in bare feet. Put on your gardening gloves,
fetch the dustpan and brush from the cellar
and sweep these pieces up quickly but carefully,
making sure you get every last sliver
from the darkest corners of the room
(later they may be held against you).
Wrap the fragments in newspaper
so no one cuts themselves.
Put back the dustpan and brush, the gloves'
upturned, amputated hands.
Make yourself a large mug of tea
with six sugars and a nip of whisky.
Stop shaking – he'll be down soon –
you can hear his alarm going off,
heavy footsteps above your head, thudding down stairs.
Stop shaking I said. Swallow this note.

Cosa Nostra

Tonight the house is steeped
as if all the windows have been stained.
It spreads silently between you
across the white steppe of tablecloth.
The bottle is open, breathing red.

It is not to be spoken of
like the old wives' cure for blemish:
raw steak rubbed into the offending flesh
then buried and left to rot.
It will be days before you leave the house.

It is both symbolic like the wine
you sipped from the lip of the chalice
kneeling before the father,
his napkin wiping clean
the smear of your defiling mouth,

and real as the wetness between
your legs that first time,
the spotting on sheet and night-dress
you caught your death in the surgical light
trying to scrub out.

Balancing Act

She is braced like glass against the air,
the fall that's always
about to happen.

The blood tilts inside her head:
in a continuous present
a girl is carrying a tumbler

towards a man lying on a bed,
limbs like a puppet flung aside.
The child is serious in her task

as a priest bearing a libation
to an unpredictable god.
This becomes her way of being good,

though daily she risks spillage,
wishes her spirit were level,
the horizon steadier in her eyes.

She tries to pull herself together,
imagines a cord tied in her guts
threading up through vertebra to cortex.

She tells herself that this is only practice:
the tightrope's laid out safely on the floor.
Though she knows in her bones

there is no rope, no floor
and some days the far side
of the kitchen is too far,

some nights the dark and sticky liquid tips
with every step she takes
across the Niagaras and canyons of the house.

Hiding Place

You were never small enough
to fit those hiding places
an animal might crawl inside
to lick its wounds, give birth –

the worn earth underneath the barn
hollowed by the shape of sleep,
the bed of needles
in the blue shadow of the pines.

And still you're nowhere near
as, choking, you flee the house
rain hissing like weak acid
against your skin, at home again

amongst the poisonous:
foxglove, nightshade, laburnum,
the tropical blooms of rhododendron
freckled like fever, throats open.

Confinement

Something is beginning to swarm –
a low frequency humming in the rafters,
the buzz of cells inside your womb.

The heat is suffocating
like the summer your nervy greyhound bitch
scratched the kitchen door to pieces,

and you were in your bedroom cramming quotes,
fist sticking to the pages of the final act:
a wife smothered by the weight of feathers.

Tonight you are disturbed
by the secret telegraphs of wasps.
The harvest moon rises like a paper nest.

The Ring Hand

You wake trapped in complex machinery.
Cogs and flesh. Teeth and bone.
A slowing clock of blood.

It is both more savage and intricate
than what you've imagined in the past:
a shed skin slung on a bedpost

like a negligée,
a deft slide into a new life,
supple and gleaming.

This is survival, a mechanism
kicking in:
You don't know what you can do

until you have to
said the hard-bitten men
who'd tasted the dead on the mountainside.

Road-kill

Driving over the broken
softness of plumage and fur
reminds you of Chardin's still lives –
the priestly way he paints dead game,
tending their corpses with light.

You remember a mallard's extravagant plunge,
one orange leg strung from a hook,
head down, white throat bared,
wings fanned open as if in flight,
ecstatic as Icarus.

Or two trapped hares
laid out tenderly side by side,
formal as Romeo and Juliet
and rendered in brushstrokes so delicate
you found your hand raised to touch.

Why don't you just leave?

And what if you are lost between two lives
like the woman stepping out of her dress
to swim the border river,
who knows the harrowing cold of the water
the terror of dying nameless,
a migrant spirit driven forever
like snow on the wind?

Tonight as you strike out into darkness,
you are dispossessed and risen like the moon,
as naked and streaming as the woman
who makes it to the other side,
who hauls herself out like a fish,
to stand in the first light with nothing
but the skin on her back.

Safe House

It's so high up it makes her dizzy,
the walls are eggshell thin –
the rumble of trains, someone slamming a door
shakes her from dreams.

She can hear screaming –
a neighbour's television –
someone calling down the stairwell
as though they are lost.

She is crying again,
but this is a need she is learning to hush,
cradling her own flesh and blood,
until she is sleeping.

From here she can see the whole city:
a flyover curved like a breast-bone,
a skyscraper's honeycomb of light,
bridges flung like arms across black water.

This is where she is now –
building a new life,
alone in one small room of the night:
she feels the tower sway in the wind.

3

*Are You Homesick
for the House of Cards?*

Are You Homesick for the House of Cards?

– CHARLES SIMIC, *'School for Visionaries'*

How can you be
when you've never escaped the palace of family
where assassins hide behind tapestries
and wolfhounds are digging in the cellar?
You feel at home and sick

in your hand-me-down skin,
watching the king flushed with vintage anger
while Jack, hunch-backed by shadows,
crouches in the corner juggling bone-handled knives.
The dark glitter of this game

keeps the queen sleeved in grief,
her tears twinned in the bedroom mirror
as she locks up something
in an iron-bound chest
and throws away the key.

You dream of teeth grinding
in a rusted lock, of leaving one night
by the secret staircase, with nothing
but a small warmth held tight beneath your cloak,
red and beating.

La Patience 1943

(after Balthus)

She only meant to play one game.
Years later she's locked in combat,
body bent double over the baize
casting her hearts into shadow.

This posture could prove mortal –
blood needling in her veins
as she cuts and deals by candlelight
the cards' lineage of pitch and flame.

She knows so many kinds of patience,
ways of contriving to get out –
the workings of each jewelled hand
are intricate as feudal saga.

The red queen covers the black king:
already her house is courting the blaze,
her daughter is in the knot garden
digging a grave for her stones.

Foundling

Each of us sleeps with a token of love:
a yellowing letter, a hazelnut shell.

Mine is half a queen's head from a thrupenny bit,
broken and bright as the winter you left me.

One day I will pluck your flesh from the air
like a magician his dove:

for now it is enough that I name you
kin to this silence, the gist of frost,

to know in the night you stand at your window
wearing the other half of the moon.

Superimposed

I feel their faces shift
beneath my own
like plates of glass –
blurring my skin to mist,
buzzing my hair to a shadowy halo.
My lips are smudged
to shyness, indecision.

I attempt to grasp,
beneath these sliding planes of flesh,
something essential – a bone structure
like the struts of a skyscraper exposed.
But my image always softens,
spongy as knuckles boiled for stock,
as the spine of a tinned salmon.

I try for definition:
foundation fixes a daily mask,
lipstick seals a singular mouth.
At work I make minute adjustments
like a dancer's fine-tuning of gesture:
to the tilt of my head, the exact
calibration of my smile.

But this vibration's in the blood,
is what's revealed
in late-night mirrors:
my face hand-held
and shaken in the dark,
my eyes like tunnels
going a long way back.

Print

This must be her, this child caught
half-crouched at the margin of a sea
that may be coming in or going out.

Her back's turned to the camera
and she seems to be focussed
on something just in front of her:

a razor shell perhaps, or worm-cast,
or simply the sheen of wet sand
mirroring the sky's empty sepia.

Further out, where the breakers whiten
the horizon lists slightly as if
the sea itself were beginning to sink.

There's nothing else in the picture,
not even the shadow
of whoever's taking it,

nothing to suggest who she might be,
this girl at the brink
of a summer's long exposure.

Vermeer's Milk Maid

I want to steal this picture –
the stillness of the girl's averted face
as she concentrates on a ribbon of milk,
oblivious of my presence.

This is a moment of balance,
like the rounded belly of the pitcher
hefted in her palm, the endless shift
of weight from vessel to vessel.

It's like observing someone at prayer –
my mother framed in the misted kitchen window,
her eyes closed and no way of knowing
what it was she was asking for.

Stitching Time

As a girl you could run up anything –
a silk blouse out of this moonlight
with intricate darts and tucks, creamy
and unpuckered as your skin was then.

But by the time I could make a decent fist
of sewing on a button, you'd stopped;
except for chain-stitched initials on my breast,
name tags tacked to the back of my neck.

Your skill was legendary as your wedding dress
until the morning I woke to the Singer's mantra
and watched you treadle bright rivers of cloth
beneath the flashing needle.

You mastered the fabric of wounds and laughter,
hemming curtains the colour of wine
that you would hang against the night,
unveiling each morning's plaque of sunlight like a queen.

You tried to teach me how to thread this beast
I'm still afraid of – with its hooks and eyes, its jabbing insatiable beak.
But you went to pieces, your fingers becoming all thumbs.
Some knowledge is only patterned in our veins,

or perhaps it's just the magic we weave
when no one's looking: a realm of lips
as red as blood, an endless beauty dreaming –
like my car running seamlessly through the dark,

or this woman walking past me on the stairs,
a swathe of material draped in her arms
like a long evening dress, like the velvet weight
of a daughter fallen asleep.

Stole

I am clumsy as a cub in your fur,
teeth and claws from your winter wardrobe.
I am practising my growl
as I stand at your mirror, mouth clownish,
lipstick clutched in my hot, little paw.

Your arms are long and swanky as gloves
as your headlights sweep the house,
catching out a glassy stare
that reflects you greenly for a second
then slips through a hole in the night.

I kick off your heels, run for my bed
where my steady breathing tries to deceive you.
Next morning the lawn is trimmed with white feathers:
all day I'm looking over my shoulder
for the eyes in the back of my dream.

Blackout '79

The strike is wildcat
plunging the house into stone-age night.
She feels for the white fingers
of wax, lights a wick –
her face leaps out of the forest,
cheekbone and socket,
flame dancing in her eyes.

This calls for a sacrifice –
meat chopped and sizzling in the pot
over the camping stove's
hissing blue crown.
It doesn't look much to appease the gods:
The King of mushroom clouds,
Keeper of the brightest light in the world.

After supper we hunker by the fire
our spines to the cold.
Now she might knit socks for the dead,
or sing me the saga of her life,
she might dip her finger into blood,
daub flocked walls with horned beasts,
or drip a cross onto our front door.

In the winter blackout
pickets howl at the scabs.
A leader is sending the army in.
A man in a white lab coat
moves the big hand closer to midnight:
time to fish out needles of bone,
start stitching our skins together.

British Winter Time

My mother moved through the house like a priest
performing a secret ritual –
touching clock hands, time's pale moon face.

In the stillness of the first October frost
I listened to midnight chiming twice.
Tomorrow would smell of windfalls and coal.

The next evening seemed biblical –
the sun set at five like a huge blood orange,
night swept over us with its feathers of soot.

The women agreed on saving light:
my grandmother, snow-haired, bitter,
peering at the television's blizzard,

her daughter, candlelit in the kitchen,
muttering *interference* as she skinned and sliced:
thighs, breasts, wings for the great chest freezer.

Winter is a spell cast under the breath,
sheets of ice that cover me still,
these hands unwinding me in the dark.

Growing a Girl

At her hand I learned to feast –
platefuls of bacon and glistening eggs,
tinned tomatoes pooled in bowls,
King Edwards big as babies' heads
borne from the cave-cold cellar.
I got everything down my neck
as if she were fattening me up for winter.

As a growing girl she'd known slaughter –
her father torn to pieces at the Somme,
her mother nourishing grievance ever after
feeding on the best at breakfast, dinner, tea,
sucking the sweet flesh of the Easter lamb,
hooking out the marrow with a skewer
until her face shone with grease.

Gran had iron in her hungry blood.
She remembered all the old cuts –
brisket, oxtail, trotters, tripe,
liver, kidney, heart, tongue.
She prepared those dark and savoury meats
with knowledge culled from grief and war:
she skinned a rabbit when she put me to sleep.

Firelighter

There's a secret to laying a fire:
the night before her fingers are black with print.
Business. Property. Appointments. Money.
Everything twisted and ready to burn.
The tongues are only sleeping.

There's a secret to lighting a fire:
a girl rises early back in the mists
rubbing her stick-thin bones together.
She's learnt the trick of sealing the hearth with paper,
the risk of holding a sheet of flame.

There's a secret to feeding a fire:
she knows when the spark has truly caught,
watches words smoke, begin to be eaten.
The kindling takes like anger,
she stokes the seasoned heartwood till it roars.

There's a secret to keeping it burning all winter:
before she retires a white-haired woman
banks up the coals until they glow
hot enough to hatch a dragon,
blankets them with whispering ashes.

I blow on them now:
the fire sucks its breath and draws.
Kneeling in the red-leaded dawn
I feel the warmth unhinge my palms
like opening wings or a prayer.

Elsie's Moon

The fuller, the better
for your waning sight.
There was a beautiful moon last night
you'd tell us, over and over

like the first line of a story –
the rest you couldn't remember.
We'd nod and agree, smiling absentmindedly
as if humouring a child.

Tonight your favourite's rising
clear of the horizon;
a birthday balloon set free
by wishing fingers

and I can see you gazing upwards
as if at a face
whose light you trust,
whose name might still come back to you.

Motherland

You smuggled out some valuables –
snatches of song, odd turns of phrase,
the lost vocabulary of weaving.

Like most exiles you brought old recipes along –
a know-how with offal,
an instinct for native fruits in their season.

You carried your hunger everywhere
zipped up in the belly of your leather bag
with those other war-time essentials –

Victory Vs and Mint Imperials for your quinsy throat,
initialled hankies for the tears you kept for best,
some Lily of the Valley cologne.

You kept to your traditional dress,
the one-to-wash, one-to-wear skirts and blouses
and greasy hats you never left the house without.

You hid more personal effects under the floorboards,
wore gloves to handle your husband's
fine singing voice and delicate face

and every Sunday you'd unwrap
from rags of chamois and jeweller's cloths
some polished fragments of your father.

How many borders you crossed, grandmother
to find yourself staring up at me –
a visitor from another world

with my exotic customs and alien music,
my brash fashions, extravagant waste,
the outlandish freedoms I did my best to hide.

Soon it will be my turn to sit up late
at the scarred kitchen table
stitching linings with the heads of queens,

to leave in the night with all I can carry –
bread and wine for the journey,
these memories, warm and heavy as a child.

At the parrot sanctuary

our presence disturbs their sleep:
heads bob and weave,
beaks biting the wire.

Some have plucked the feathers
from their tails,
their breasts,
as if trying to find out love.

Bright eyes stare out
from circles of wizened skin,
fix us,

and then the dead begin to speak:

a chorus of greetings and goodbyes,
nicknames, profanities,
the ghost of a woman's laugh.

No one can live long
with this ventriloquy,
voices thrown from the dark.

Not us,
who leave them quickly to their cages,
to the silence that only comes
when we are gone.